AT Y

CONVENIENCE

PUBLIC TOILETS FROM
AROUND THE WORLD

EBURY
PRESS

1 3 5 7 9 10 8 6 4 2

All images copyright © CORBIS
Compilation © Ebury Press

First published 2001 by Ebury Press,
an imprint of Random House,
20 Vauxhall Bridge Road, London SW1V 2SA
www.randomhouse.co.uk

Random House Australia (Pty) Limited
20 Alfred Street, Milsons Point, Sydney,
New South Wales 2061, Australia

Random House New Zealand Limited
18 Poland Road, Glenfield, Auckland 10, New Zealand

Random House South Africa (Pty) Limited
Endulini, 5a Jubilee Road, Parktown 2193, South Africa

The Random House Group Limited Reg. No. 954009

Printed and bound in China by C&C Offset Printing Co., Ltd

A CIP catalogue record for this book is available from the British Library.

ISBN 0 09 188302 4

Pee at your peril – an official dictate photographed
in Bhutan.
© *David Samuel Robbins/CORBIS*

AT YOUR CONVENIENCE – PUBLIC TOILETS FROM AROUND THE WORLD
EBURY PRESS · www.randomhouse.co.uk

His and Hers Amish-style – restrooms in Lancaster, Pennsylvania, USA.
© *Roman Soumar/CORBIS*

AT YOUR CONVENIENCE – PUBLIC TOILETS FROM AROUND THE WORLD
EBURY PRESS · www.randomhouse.co.uk

Big Brother is watching – "toilet paper must be used by order of the administration", Cuenca, Ecuador.
© *Owen Franken/CORBIS*

AT YOUR CONVENIENCE – PUBLIC TOILETS FROM AROUND THE WORLD

EBURY PRESS · www.randomhouse.co.uk

The dreaded country fair portaloo seen here at the
Kildysart Agricultural Show, County Clare, Ireland.
© Michael St Maur Sheil/CORBIS

Women waiting for their menfolk at a public convenience
sponsored by local business in Varanasi, India.
© *Jeremy Horner/CORBIS*

AT YOUR CONVENIENCE – PUBLIC TOILETS FROM AROUND THE WORLD
EBURY PRESS · www.randomhouse.co.uk

Nature's flush – a traditional Nepali toilet constructed
over a stream. Photographed at Bagarchap in the
Annapurna region of the Himalayas.
© Galen Rowell/CORBIS

AT YOUR CONVENIENCE – PUBLIC TOILETS FROM AROUND THE WORLD
EBURY PRESS · www.randomhouse.co.uk

A surfer outside the men's toilet at a beach
in Peru, 1980.
© *Tony Arruza/CORBIS*

AT YOUR CONVENIENCE – PUBLIC TOILETS FROM AROUND THE WORLD
EBURY PRESS · www.randomhouse.co.uk

Pull up a seat – the St Lucia tourist board welcome you
to one of their facilities in the Windward Islands.
© *Earl & Nazima Kowall/CORBIS*

AT YOUR CONVENIENCE – PUBLIC TOILETS FROM AROUND THE WORLD
EBURY PRESS · www.randomhouse.co.uk

The oasis – a Namibian public toilet, Fish River Canyon.
© *Edifice/CORBIS*

Don't fancy yours much – decrepit rural facilities found
along the Alaska Highway, USA.
© George Lepp/CORBIS

AT YOUR CONVENIENCE – PUBLIC TOILETS FROM AROUND THE WORLD
EBURY PRESS · www.randomhouse.co.uk

Chickens kept in a toilet in Changsha, China.
© David H Wells/CORBIS

AT YOUR CONVENIENCE – PUBLIC TOILETS FROM AROUND THE WORLD
EBURY PRESS · www.randomhouse.co.uk

Never caught out – Japanese baseball fans at the
Fukuoka Dome watch the game on small televisions as
they use the urinals.
© Michael S Yamashita/CORBIS

AT YOUR CONVENIENCE – PUBLIC TOILETS FROM AROUND THE WORLD
EBURY PRESS · www.randomhouse.co.uk

"Omen" – the women's restroom behind a Mennonite
church in Waynesboro, Pennsylvania, USA.
© *Raymond Gehman/CORBIS*

AT YOUR CONVENIENCE – PUBLIC TOILETS FROM AROUND THE WORLD
EBURY PRESS · www.randomhouse.co.uk

"Have you paid and displayed?" – unintentional humour at a car park loo in Goring, England.
© *Chris Andrews Publications/CORBIS*

AT YOUR CONVENIENCE – PUBLIC TOILETS FROM AROUND THE WORLD
EBURY PRESS · www.randomhouse.co.uk

An old public urinal sign in Lisbon, Portugal.
© *KM Westermann/CORBIS*

Toilets at the local railroad station in Arvi, India.
© *Milepost 92 1/2 /CORBIS*

AT YOUR CONVENIENCE – PUBLIC TOILETS FROM AROUND THE WORLD
EBURY PRESS · www.randomhouse.co.uk

AT YOUR CONVENIENCE – PUBLIC TOILETS FROM AROUND THE WORLD

EBURY PRESS · www.randomhouse.co.uk

An elderly Paris Metro restroom attendant stands
at her post.

AT YOUR CONVENIENCE – PUBLIC TOILETS FROM AROUND THE WORLD

EBURY PRESS · www.randomhouse.co.uk

The remains of the public toilets amid the ancient ruins of Ephesus, Turkey. For the Ancient Greeks going to the loo was a sociable event.

© Richard T Nowitz/CORBIS

AT YOUR CONVENIENCE – PUBLIC TOILETS FROM AROUND THE WORLD
EBURY PRESS · www.randomhouse.co.uk

The Westerner's worst nightmare – a hole-in-the-ground
"squat" toilet in Dehra Doon, India.
© *Earl & Nazima Kowall/CORBIS*

AT YOUR CONVENIENCE – PUBLIC TOILETS FROM AROUND THE WORLD
EBURY PRESS · www.randomhouse.co.uk

With modern art it's hard to know which is which –
toilet signage in the aptly named Kakadu National Park,
Northern Territory, Australia.

Putting out the fire – outdoor urinals below a movie
billboard in New Dehli, India.
© David & Peter Turnley/CORBIS

AT YOUR CONVENIENCE – PUBLIC TOILETS FROM AROUND THE WORLD
EBURY PRESS · www.randomhouse.co.uk

Nun on the run – pilgr　　using portable toilets at
Conyers Wait, Georgia, U
© *Ed Kashi/CORBIS*

AT YOUR CONVENIENCE – PUBLIC TOILETS FROM AROUND THE WORLD
EBURY PRESS • www.randomhouse.co.uk

Rock and toilet roll – cubicles over the cesspit at the
Glastonbury Festival, Somerset, England.
© *Rune Hellestad/CORBIS*

Advertising the latest hardware – a billboard in
Kerala, India.
© *Sheldan Collins/CORBIS*

His and Hers signage in local costume in Himachel
Pradesh, India.
© David Samuel Robbins/CORBIS (detail)

AT YOUR CONVENIENCE – PUBLIC TOILETS FROM AROUND THE WORLD
EBURY PRESS · www.randomhouse.co.uk